Poems & Prayers

Also by Matthew McConaughey
Greenlights

POEMS

&

PRAYERS

MATTHEW
McCONAUGHEY

HEADLINE

First published in the US in 2025 by Crown Publishing Group
A division of Penguin Random House LLC

First published in the UK in 2025 by Headline Publishing Group Limited

5

Cataloguing in Publication Data is available from the British Library

Hardback ISBN 978 1 0354 0554 1
Trade Paperback ISBN 978 1 0354 3796 2

Offset in 11/16 pt Tribute OT by Six Red Marbles UK, Thetford, Norfolk

Printed and bound in India by Manipal Technologies Limited

MIX
Paper | Supporting
responsible forestry
FSC
www.fsc.org   FSC™ C104740

Headline Publishing Group Limited
An Hachette UK Company
Carmelite House
50 Victoria Embankment
London EC4Y 0DZ

The authorised representative in the EEA is Hachette Ireland,
8 Castlecourt Centre, Dublin 15, D15 XTP3, Ireland (email: info@hbgi.ie)

www.headline.co.uk
www.hachette.co.uk

Dedicated to the original dream, belief.

CONTENTS

Poems & Prayers

INTRODUCTION

To make song of the spoken word and
music of the melody of life.

To put rhyme to the rhythm of the hands of time.

---

*"It is [a poet's] privilege to help man endure by lifting his
heart, by reminding him of the courage and honor and
hope and pride and compassion and pity and sacrifice
which have been the glory of his past. The poet's voice need
not merely be the record of man, it can be one of the props,
the pillars to help him endure and prevail."*

—William Faulkner

---

*"To give voice to a language of the soul that
encourages a like response from others."*

—*Daily Word*, July 13, 1996

---

it's all a poem,
if the letters in the alphabet are in a certain order.

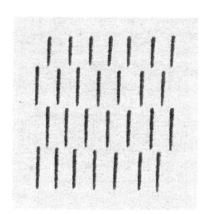

I'VE ALWAYS RELIED ON LOGIC TO MAKE SENSE OF
MYSELF AND THE WORLD.

A prescriptionist at heart, I've always looked to reason to
find the rhyme, the practical to get to the mystical, the
choreography to find the dance, the proof to get to the truth,
and reality to get to the dream. I've always believed that art
emulates life, not the other way around.

I've been finding that tougher to do lately.

Seems to me the *facts* have become unreliably overrated.

So many of us today are out to prove that the truth is just an
outdated nostalgic notion, that honesty, along with being
correct and *right,* is now a deluded currency in our cultural
economy. With an epidemic of half-cocked logic and illusions
being sold as sound conclusions, it's more than hard to know
what to believe in; it's hard to believe.

But I don't want to quit believing, and I don't want to stop
believing *in* . . . humanity, you, myself, our potential.

I'm not ready to concede that entertainment and
misinformation are now our garden of knowledge. That lies are
just *what we tell each other,* especially ourselves. That trust is no
longer the coin of the realm. That doubt's worth more than
hope. That there's no difference between dreams and illusions.

I'm not ready for my conscience to retreat. I'm not ready to accept that reality's not enough.

In our age of politics, AI, plastic surgery, and high-frequency fix-it-in-post deepfake deceptions, I often find myself walking away from all the *knowledge* and *reality* more confused, more frustrated, and less well-advised than I was before I consumed it.

As a people, we don't seem to be perceiving properly, which means we are not desiring properly, which means we aren't understanding properly, and as long as we don't understand properly, we're not going to act properly.

Like most all of us, I'm trying to navigate and adapt as shrewdly as I can to our changing times. To understand where I fit in, where I don't, define what I stand for, and what I won't. But I find myself increasingly tempted to just *settle* for the false and profane as acceptable signs of our times.

Should I maintain a beginner's mind and continue to seek the magic in life when the facts deny reason to do so?

How do I stave off the cynics' disease and still remain a hopeful skeptic?

Are we hoping to survive or surviving to hope?

Maybe that's the point.

To admit that evil is necessary, and choose to rise above it—or not.

To admit the ugly facts and untruths all around and inside us, and *still* believe.

I think that is the point.

As an optimist and a believer, I'm a man of strong spirit and great faith, but if it's belief we seek, let's admit it: we're not going to find it looking to the evidence.

So, enough with the academic and mathematic equations that aren't adding up. I think it's time for us to flip the script on

what's historically been our means of making sense, and instead
open our aperture to enchantment and look to faith, belief, and
dreams for our reality.

Let's sing more than we might make sense, believe in more
than the world can conclude, get more impressed with the wow
instead of the how, let inspiration interrupt our appointments,
dream our way to reality, serve some soul food to our hungry
heads, put proof on the shelf for a season, and rhyme our way
to reason. Forget logic, certainty, owning, or making a start-up
company of it; let's go beyond what we can merely imagine,
and believe, in the poetry of life.

MUSICAL BRIDGES FROM THE MUNDANE,
POEMS ARE A SATURDAY IN THE MIDDLE OF THE WEEK.
THEY ILLUMINATE BELIEF,
INVITING NEW WAYS TO SEEK.
POEMS ARE SONGS OF ROMANCE,
WITH OURSELVES, OTHERS, SPACE, PLACE, AND TIME.
HYMNS OF HOLY LANGUAGE,
ANGELIC DITTIES OF THE DIVINE,
POEMS ARE ALSO PRAYERS,
THAT RHYME.

For me, **prayer** is a time to reset, to catch my breath, and
get a spiritual yawn of acceptance and surrender before my
call to action. I pray as a means of staying involved in my life
and the life of those I love and care for. Prayer anchors me but
doesn't hold me down, giving me a more stable floor from
which to fly from. As a proclivity to imitate the divine, the

high-mindedness of prayer guides us to a place of intentional surrender that promises more than permission, but freedom. Prayer can also be a scream, a plea, a question, an expression of pain and longing, or a therapeutic means of facing a monster within us.

The origin of prayer is based on **worship,** where and when we have the humility to bend low and bow, to raise our heart above our head, so we can listen to the wisdom of the sacred within us. But prayer isn't solely sequestered to ceremony in the synagogues, churches, and meccas of the world. Prayer may also come in the form of meditation, taking a walk to clear your mind, stargazing to feel the humility of awe, creating art, making love, writing, even laughter. All of these practices can be a form of prayer because they're each a means of revival—of the heart, mind, and the human spirit.

Prayer is **paying attention.** In a world that constantly consumes our thoughts but distracts us from tending to our spirit, prayer gives our soul a chance to catch up with our pathologically busy minds, providing us with the contentment of self-awareness that gives us enough hope to admit that we actually do have the ability to live our life. In times of chaos, prayer **restores order,** and regardless of the higher power you're praying to, a committed belief in our continued improvement is how we first restore order in ourselves.

In a society that suffers from the illusion that privation and possessions equal *progress,* prayer promotes what I believe is a more genuine definition of the word: the development of human potential to become a broadcaster and receiver of values. Because prayer intentionally aligns us with what we value most, the practice of prayer *is* **progress.**

The ultimate goal of prayer is to align our earthly ambitions to be in accordance with Divinity's Law. This means believing in more than who we are, but rather in who we can be. Through the inherent tests and approvals of our highest order, prayer helps us discover what we are here to do in this life. And when we can live more in sync with our higher power's will? We've found what is theological code for our **purpose.**

More love affair than mandate, prayer is devotion more than responsibility. Devoid of the false idols of our superstitions, prayer is a moral yearning to our own elevated conscience. The pattern and practice of prayer starts as a secret, then becomes a conscious light on the path that shows us the way to becoming our more competent and true selves.

Personally, I begin my prayers with gratitude.

I smile upon my blessings.

I try to humble my selfish desires.

I remember that in God's economy, service serves me.

I pray for the guidance to do all that I can as a husband and father for the mental, physical, and spiritual health of my family.

Then I take a scroll down the Rolodex of my memory's lane and take inventory of all those I love and care for in my life, until I see them with my mind's eye at a time when they were most themselves.

Not happiest or most proud, not saddest or most reflective.

But when they were no one else but themselves and their light shone brightest.

When they were in their own state of Grace, satisfied and content.

That's when I lock in on this image of them in my mind, and pray for *that* in them, in perpetuity.

Next comes what is often the hardest part, trying to see

myself the same way. But I pray until I do, rolling through the frames of my own past until a true image of myself becomes clear.

Then I concentrate on that likeness, embrace it, thank it, and open up to letting it fill me.

Then I say, amen.

LIKE TWO HANDS IN WORSHIP
POEMS AND PRAYERS INTERLACE,
DANCING WITH OUR SOUL IN SONG,
TO THE MUSIC WE MUST FACE.
I WRITE POETRY BECAUSE I BELIEVE LIFE RHYMES,
FOR MORE MEANING IS WHY I PRAY,
AND WHEN THE RHYME MATTERS AND THE MEANING'S
IN VERSE,
IT'S A HEAVEN-SENT PARLAY.

My prayers are my poems
are my prayers.

And the following is four
decades of poems and
prayers I've written since
I was eighteen, back when
I started reading Byron in
the bathtub in Australia.

This is a poem I wrote right after I finished writing *Greenlights* and later included in the paperback edition. It's a chronological summary of everything that happens in that book. So if you read it, I think you'll have some fun remembering what spoke to you. And if you didn't read the whole damn book, here's the five-minute version.

GREENLIGHTS
INTERMEZZO

We're all gonna die, our eulogy will introduce
    us when we're gone.
So how are we gonna live a life we look forward
    to looking back at?
How are we gonna make life a greenlight?
Seems to be about
wants and needs
skill and timing
responsibility and fate
getting relative with the inevitable; persist,
    pivot, or concede.
We'll fight and make up,
answer to our name, love, tell the truth, and
    just do it.

We'll sit, and talk, and listen
initiated through rites of passage.
We'll learn fundamentals before raising our
    freak flags,
confront to unify.
We might have to piss for our present,
and piss our pants in fear,
threaten someone to save our ass,
structure our freedom,
show our dough,
teach to understand,
work hard,
perform CPR,
build treehouses,
lose lawsuits,
put bullshit on a bumpersticker,
defend our dad,
trade in red sports cars,
get rid of who we're not to find out who we
    are,
keep handshake deals and choose to be
    culturally different on principle,
face the future,
choose a path,
and not half-ass it.
With innate ability and effort
we'll tuck our shirt back in,
make the grades to get the experience,
we'll travel,
find common denoms of values in mankind,
celebrate our differences,

walk in the right bar,
get inspired by our heroes,
be cool and prosper.
We'll lose loved ones and never let them die,
we'll grow up, and keep them alive.
It will take undeniable steam,
our timing will be off sometimes,
we will chase the unknown and need it too
    much,
then receive gifts from strangers
on the autobahn,
where the first time's a charm,
we KNOW it.
Bet it all and fail,
lose things where we left them,
and find them later on,
because we can,
even if we didn't want to.
We'll overthink it,
wing it,
embarrass ourselves,
make outlandish plans and pull them off,
we'll get lucky,
call our mom,
make the moment,
be thankful and still,
choke under pressure,
believe it all,
get famous for something,
get wobbly and lost,
then go away to pray,

and realize it's all a paradox.
We'll parent our parents,
and challenge the order,
have beautiful nightmares,
chase them down alone,
wrestle with our demons,
until we quit looking,
and see the truth,
where what we want and need
is right in front of us.
Forgetting more than we learned and
    remembering more than we knew,
it takes work either way.
We'll rent many places,
where privileged prayers and necessary
    devotions
get lost in the haze,
have proof of our innocence,
and still get arrested.
We'll get bailed out,
be folk heroes,
have hangovers
and have to skip town,
we'll stay in the game, kiss the fire and walk
    away whistlin',
we'll pick a fight with God,
lose our hair,
tiptoe through the raindrops,
make our own rules, break them,
and our beautiful nightmare will return,
calling us to chase it down again.

Where we'll step in wet shit to be remembered,
and wrestle in the sand,
not about right or wrong,
we'll try to understand.
We'll touch the divine then spit in our own face.
So our nose will always know we left our scent,
we'll act blind and we won't see,
the justice it deserves.
We'll run in the sun and swim in the sea,
and break all kinds of sweats,
being good at what we don't love,
we'll be a fraud,
get restless,
and turn the page again,
have another wet dream,
that allows us to forgive,
then we'll meet the one,
kidnap and keep her,
move into small spaces together to be closer,
upset mommas,
and prefer to leave the lights on,
doing one thing at a time.
Somebody will get sick and life will need more
    care,
the honeymoon over,
we look in the mirror and see our stare,
no more lookin' over our shoulder,
we bet on ourself,
and become the one thing we always wanted
    to be.
We'll make babies,

and now with a life to sacrifice,
we'll risk losing the fight.
Hearing our ancestors sing
we'll get selfish,
and instead of chasing ourself,
we start hunting us down,
making promises we keep,
we take the leap,
hoping to fly until it's time to land,
memory catches up,
we see the future, and it's just like you knew it
    would be.
Time and truth proved again,
fuck the bucks, go for the win,
don't ask permission, don't flinch when they
    swing,
you now know what you knew,
you're back in the ring.
You'll drive the same highway back and both
    ways again.
Except this time you run your race in the game,
there is no crisis at all,
you go undefeated, no loss, all gain,
and win the gold trophy,
when they call your name.
You chased your hero, you hunted him down,
now, it's time to catch him.
To predate the prey.
To catch your breath, and set him in your
    sights,

a mortal man he will be no more, the match is
    all but over.
But before you pull the trigger you gotta catch
    him,
and change the game.
So you can chase your hero all over again.
It's all relative, except the inevitable,
and you know me, I never want it to end.
Amen.
just keep livin', greenlights.

NAVIGATION

&

LIVIN'

DITTIES

Navigation is a compass to help guide our way. We navigate to get out of trouble, to find the path forward, to remain on our way.

Ditties are songs, the written beat poetry of assembled circumstances that naturally convene in real time to make a story, that's sometimes worth singing. Some mornings I wake up with a certain musical meter in my mind. If I like the sound of it, I'll do my best to move to the pace of that rhythm throughout the day, to exchange the cadence with everything I see and do. If I keep that meter in the way I think, see, and move, the world around me often responds in kind to my calling, making every interaction I have a rhyming verse in the song that is my day.

And when I'm done jotting it all down, it becomes a ditty. When our life has rhythm we can dance through it, and the struggles start to feel more like snuggles, the broken arms become bruises, and the battles end up being good luck.

Is life the chase we race
until death catches us running by?
Or are we racing death from birth
only caught the day we die?
Either way, let's hold the lead for as long as we can.

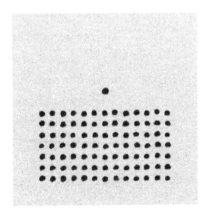

FURTHER FROM HELL

you can call them poems but what they are is lyrics
songs about a life of soaring spirits
where reason rhymes and the light's just right
where never's done and always might
where standing's sturdy in the wind's blow
and sights are high without tippy a toe
where we know for certain that we're not sure
if prevention's best medicine is the cure
when being on time is when you show
and your soul's account is flush with dough
where looking back don't hurt as much as you thought
and telling the future's as easy as ought
where forgiveness is free to give and to get
we reunite once again with people we've met
where tragedy and triumph are both words worth the giggle
the chains come off and give room to wiggle
when love stories are told in front of our eyes
believe them all they are not lies
where your back is watched while you look ahead
in no hurry but excited for the day you're dead
where it's all for nothing and everything as well
in a place called heaven further from hell.

IN MATTERS OF THE SPIRIT
I BELIEVE MORE THAN I KNOW,
THAT WHO I AM TODAY
DETERMINES WHERE I'LL GO.

SKINNY COWS AND DOLLAR BILLS.

Put 'em by the fence line
and on the outside of your money clip.

Don't advertise you got fat heifers
and Benjies on the inside.

SHADES FOR THE ECLIPSE

Headin' into town to find a girl named Nikki,
they say she's got shades for the e-clipse.

Naked eye on the sun today will surely cause quite a twitch,
Lord, lead me from temptation, with absence of a glitch.

It's a blue moon Saturday mornin' and there's treble in my breeze,
and since tomorrow's Sunday, good idea to stretch my knees.

No one's expectin' me, and nobody minds,
no need for laws when you're civil and you're kind.

All my appointments are merely suggestions,
if I'm unimpressed, I'll make the impressions.

Know where to climb cus out here's too level,
when you can see the bad guys comin', you're less afraid of the devil

This two-way traffic don't lean on yellow lines
and the burrito at the bank's worth a dollar for my dimes.

Gonna drop off the trash, get rations for my water,
write a tune for my wife, a poem for my daughter.

Oops, took a quick peek at the sky before I got my glasses,
now I can't see shit, sure hope this passes.

Good thing I got on my GPS,
cus this drivin' half blind is a hell of a test.

Takin' my time, cruise control doin' eighty
to see the e-clipse where it's gonna get shady.

Best rest while I'm up, sleep on the job later,
cus when the moon serves the sun it's time to tip the waiter.

I'm headin' into town to find a girl named Nikki,
they say she's got shades for the e-clipse.

This is one of those ditties that made my day
into a song. It all happened, including buying
a no-tax two-buck burrito from a lady who
had set up a stove in an abandoned bank.
One of the best burritos I've ever had.

CHANGING LANES

(preferably read to the rhythm of ZZ Top's '72 jam "Just Got Paid")

I just got paid today, I got myself a pocket full of change,
no need to use my blinker now when I'm changing lanes.

These hogs on the highway are not here to measure speed,
I have everything I want and it's exactly what I need.

I have a round-trip invitation to the left of these yellow lines,
don't need no reservations, I'm welcome anytime.

Up ahead's an open road and over my shoulder is self-stated,
where the last hope wins and memory's overrated.

My check doesn't need a sign, it's already been cashed,
as I sneak in the front door with no hide in my stash.

Appreciate the pace but don't dare be in a hurry,
keep your windshield clean so your vision won't get blurry.

Run too fast to get there early's gonna make you late tomorrow,
show up now for future dates, today's time you will borrow.

Ahead or behind it, time questions what we know,
pace your feet to your own beat and on it you will show.

Try to catch your breath with everyone you take,
forgiving to forget with every yawn you make.

It's okay to be scared but do not be afraid,
racing these rats to beat 'em is a bed you already made.

When your sword must be drawn, commit to the grip,
and when you speak in tongue, don't let it slip.

When the mark's not met to the plans that you made,
reschedule your dream until the bill gets paid.

When your mind is wet and humid and your heart is just as
    gray,
whistle in the breeze to hold the storm at bay.

When the lights go out at night and your head lays down to rest,
Rolodex your days, worse, better, and the best.

The fact that you give grade is how you will improve,
honest self-assessments dance us back into our groove.

Cus if you shoot for an A and end up with a B,
it's worth more than an F when you tried to make a C.

Be best at what you're good at not better at what you're not,
win again at what you won at before you fight with what you
    fought.

When certainty is clear, and your sight is just as valid,
thank the garden of knowledge for the greens in your salad.

And when more than you could imagine exceeds your
    expectation,
bet on and believe it's more than a vacation.

When the company's enjoyed alone and with yourself,
and you can but don't want to be with anyone else.

Congratulate the mirror cus you've just pulled off a coup,
now get out there and practice being good at being you.

Where none of it matters and nothing's in vain,
there's no need to use your blinker when you're changing lanes.

DEUCES

Forty miles south of Poteet,
looking for a lid to rest my seat
with my stomach in knots,
my prostate in a pinch,
the clock was ticking,
I was grumpy as a grinch.
With the sun now rising,
just past six a.m.
found a roadside loo,
and I went on in.
I passed the janitor
who was on his way out,
which gave me faith
and relieved my doubt.
See, I consider a porta-potty
an absolute win
long as the first butt in the mornin's mine
on the porce-lin.

... another ditty written in real time

Covet nothing but your superior self.
Seek transformation over transaction.
Individuality over conformity.
Recognize your inadequacies.
Then make one step at a time in the right direction and endure.
It will be harder than you think.
Because your long road has no arrival.
Until you die.

This was inspired by Judges **17:6** in the Bible, with
some Texas Ranger giddy-up justice mixed in.

LIFE ON THE RISE

It's evolution without solution
Where belief's worth more than a conclusion.

A verb of passage not a noun of pro
A revival seeking testament till we get where we go.

So act like you care even if you don't.
And when it's time, jump before you fall.

CANON.

Sellin' Sunday morning like Saturday night,
Gotta pay the tithe if we wanna get the right.
Drink some clean water under the neon light,
A hickey on your neck minus the bite.

There's gospel music playing here at the rave,
How we gonna dance in the home of the brave?
A little bit of duty with a touch of Dutch,
Gonna cost us everything but not that much.

CHOOSE.
Time to sell, before we negotiate,
Evangelize, don't administrate.
Own to rent before we rent to own.
Don't sell yourself short, get overshown.

Trust in God but don't rely on fate,
Look in the mirror, meet your mate.
Make a movement over a magistrate,
Where getting married's just one long date.

BELIEVE.
Opportunities over obligations,
We take care of ourselves we take care of the nations.
Turn your light on and flick your switch,
Keep faith in the dark, demonstrate, don't bitch.

Remember now don't forget what we're in,
Revolution's only rebellion until you win.
The future's on the table and there for the taking,
Get what you give, it's here for the making.

DO.
How to build better people is in your reflection.
Take more credit, make the connection.
Earn your currency, spend it well,
A useful story's worth the tell.

Don't find yourself, be the creation,
The pursuit is all, there's no destination.
Know who you're not, commit to the chase,
It's an infinite game, stay in the race.

TRUST.
Heard and purchased, in sight and seen.
Getting out of the haze and into the dream.
Be on time, not ahead or behind it,
Quit lookin' around and just fuckin' find it.

Your freedom is responsible for us.
Invest in yourself, so we all ride the bus.

I've filled four passports and put **400,000** miles behind an Airstream I towed around North America. I've written love songs and poems to most of the places I've been: Mali, London, New York, Cleveland, New Orleans, to name a few. This next one's about Birmingham, Alabama. I've also tried to leave every place I visited a little better than I found it. Hope I did.

BIRMINGHAM

I paid half price for the same roll of dice
I got the first time what I tried to get twice
I got fewer tickets and drove the same speed
I did what I wanted to get what I need

I traveled half as far
and I got twice as close
because what I was after
was more than the most

I bullshitted more
but told fewer lies
because the truth matters less
than the look in your eyes

I didn't find myself missing the places I'd been
where people got sick more than they sinned
I got in less fights but took more on the chin
where the only blue ribbon goes to win.

In Birmingham, where I care less but give more of a damn.

Manicured and mannered,
honored and clean,
rugged and tough
without being mean.

Red enough to work,
blue enough to dream,
like Southern royalty
without the queen.

Dressed up for the evenings,
they like to be seen,
heavy on maintenance
they leverage their lean.

A great sense of humor
not afraid to eat crow
it's Aspen in the south
without the snow.

**In Birmingham, where they care less if you give a damn,
about Birmingham.**

PLEASE REMIND ME TO GIVE
THANKS **IN** ALL CIRCUMSTANCES
NOT **FOR** ALL CIRCUMSTANCES

Time to look up to what's not yet been seen
where the dream is God and God's the dream
A place called home in the den of the belief
where the last conviction wins the crown of relief.

This one's based on the theological concept that if you believe in God, then you are supposed to be a lost and wandering immigrant on Earth. Here, you have no home, and even though you know you'll never find home here, you stay steadfast in the search. And that's the point, because even though your only home is in Heaven, if you keep trying to find and make Heaven on Earth, you'll get back home when you leave.

CAPABLY ABLE

come home, door's locked, key don't fit the hole
sneak in through the outhouse, step in the toilet bowl
eat more bananas, monkey around
next thing you know they run you outta town

crawl fast, run slow, sneak down the alleyway
pencil whip the tax man so you don't have to pay
count down tally up, your show's on the road
make enuf green to lighten your load

swing at a ball when you thought it was a strike
then the power plant dies when they hand you the mic
apologize twice for what never was a sin
get sent to jail you know the fix was in

he said, she said, down goes a domino
first one falls, then they're all gonna go
look around, what do you see?
keep your shades on if you wanna skip the fee

roundabouts, red lights, stop signs, and late nights
blacktops, dirt roads, slow-downs to keep ahold
autobahns, highways, greenlights, and byways
free to fly the friendly skies as long as you're goin' my ways

getaway to getaways, just to see the sun shine
I still want yours, even though I got mine.
shindig, dancehall, a two-step rap and a rage
how do I read the news if I can't turn the page?

alley-oops, slam dunks, Hail Marys, trick shots
gotta break the rules if you want a spoon to stir the pot
freeze frame, dynamite, stay stuck, blow it up
I love you forever so let's sign the prenup

sit down, listen up, chit chat, and de-bate
hash it out, reach around, get yourself a re-bate
reset, preset, rhythm and rock
gotta get your own before you go and get got

layoffs, furloughs, lawyers wanna depose
knots in the water hose, got another bloody nose
got your credit, debit, and diamond rings
but if you got the gold, you be the king

Yes, I woke up this morning a little wobbly and unstable
but I got chickens in the coop and breakfast on my table
good thing I can sing a tune and yarn myself a fable.
Because I may not be willing, but I'm capably able.

TIME

The big existential question. We're all trying to find more of it, save more of it, and even get ahead of it. I love to be on time, and when I am, I don't need a watch. I don't just specifically mean appointments, I mean finding a pace and frequency where I'm not tardy for anything and never have to rush.

People are always telling me *You're so laid back, so cool*. Well, that's got a lot to do with the fact that I've prepared and planned for the day ahead, which allows me to move deliberately, take my time, adapt, and saunter through the day instead of race through it.

But time and timing are about more than a day's pace. The bigger question is, how much time do we have in life? How do we manage that time? Who do we want to spend it with?

These days we have more things that supposedly allow us to be more productive in a shorter amount of time, but I feel like we're racing *against* time more than ever before. That math doesn't add up.

Our lives are so consumed with comparison selling us so many things that we think we want, but don't really need— another fad, another app, another "like." Is this what we want to do with our time? Is the race we're running about the quantity of time or the quality of it?

So many people are obsessed with how to live longer instead of how to live better. And while that may be a measure of success, it often comes at the expense of profit. I don't know about you, but I'd rather live sixty satisfying years than ninety not.

P.S. I've looked for more than twenty-four hours in many a day and I've yet to find another second.

BACKSWING

In between destruction and existence
paths of persistence and least resistance
below the climb and above the bow
where what it is answers how
when running sits still
between fate and free will.

On the other side of a mortal limit
past the gravity of any inhibit
where the truth pirouettes on stable feet
behind reaching out, ahead of retreat
where our sovereign soul is safe at home
unanimous, yet still alone.

Where the definition of evolution
is served as such in the solution.
When the context of each and every choice
only hears the sound of our own voice
salacious and still satisfied
where desires heed and never hide.

In the Kingdom of suspense and the incomplete
when not yet and already finally meet
between our getting and our give,
here in the backswing, where we're dying to live.

GREATNESS IS NOT ALL TO
EACH. IT IS EACH TO ALL.

THE GENIUS CAN DO
ANYTHING BUT DOES ONE
THING AT A TIME.

You'll find a few proverbs in this book. I like
proverbs because they're mantras and precepts that
often require an intentionally curious interpretation,
allowing us to make them our own. And while
proverbs may not rhyme in word, they sure do rhyme
in reason.

TIME TO TRADE

Quietly on main street,
in the waiting room,
on the porch,
in the vestibule on the other side of the seeing.
Under the shade below the sun,
in the sleep before my stretch,
in no rush to stay,
in no hurry to go,
I decided to stay awake with my eyes open
and dream sooner than when they closed.
Because time was a trade,
negotiable only if I wanted to keep it,
which I did not.

This was a hazy dream I had with my eyes open one
mid-September afternoon in a hammock on a shady
porch next to a Mexican saloon.

BACK TO THE FUTURE

we look ahead to where we've been
we pray so we can sin
we leave so we can go
we give back to steal the show

we raise the roof so we can hide
we rebel so we can abide
we laugh so we can cry
we find reason then ask why

we get ahead to slow down
we get high to look around
we stay up late to see the sun
we show up tardy so we can run

we smile so we can frown
we side right up to upside down
we get dirty to get clean
we hideout so we can be seen

all so we can we can go back,
to the future

To do it once more means you did it again.
To do what's never been done reveals it's always been.

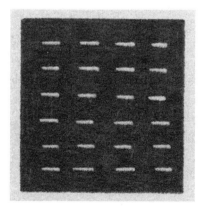

MEMORY

Unlike her cousin conscience dares
she patiently waits and always cares,
judging us not for our neural void
though we may be, she's not annoyed.

A graceful poet she finds us lost
and greets us with reflection,
she rhymes us with reminding times
so we can make the connection.

Just and true, she's déjà vu
and surprises us with chances,
she flies and floats from clouds to boats
and with our dreams she dances.

Always near and never far
she's a teacher always right behind us,
on our shoulder as we greet each day
when we take the time she's right beside us.

Memory never forgets.
Even though we do.

I'M NOT SURE WHAT THE
OBSESSION WITH MY
MEMORY'S ABOUT.

I WAS THERE.

BARBITURATE LOGIC

I need to calm my brain to have half the thoughts per hour.
50% of the neural fragments.
And therefore twice the power.
And one doubly meaningful story with half the words.

TWICE THE TIME.

Living in my future and missing my past,
racing against time instead of making it last.
Like a moment ahead's gonna double up the past one,
and an hour later's gonna make up for the last one.
This showing up early's just as late of a fix,
as 8 is to 4 when the truth's at 6.
Just feels like this dying is a one-way debit,
so I'm getting ahead to find equal credit.

WITHOUT COMPLACENCY,
TRUST THAT TIME IS ON YOUR SIDE.

Proverbs provide clear direction in the storm.

TIME AND TRUTH.

TWO CONSTRAINTS YOU
CAN RELY ON.

ONE ALWAYS SHOWS UP,
THE OTHER NEVER LEAVES.

Proverbs are also spiritual math
equations of cause and effect based
on observations and life experiences.

KARMIC GRACE

The golden rule of Karmic grace is that
    when we do no good unto others,
they will do no good unto us,
and when we do good unto others,
they may not do good unto us,
but the laws of the universe will.

MORE TIME

Think it was about 2 a.m.
the band played their last tune and I said amen.
Went to pay my tab over at the bar,
when the main event started tuning their guitar.
So I ordered myself another bottle of wine,
God I love it when I got more time.

Thought it was the year two thousand and ten,
not a worry in sight in the fast lane again.
Signed all my checks one year tardy,
because it was '09 and I hadn't left the party.
So happy my balance wasn't in the red,
God I love it when I'm early instead.

Met a woman I liked and she became my friend,
we turned into lovers thought we'd make it until the end.
But as soon as we lined up hand in hand in the queue,
my eyes started turning a lighter shade of blue.
Sometimes love just loses its shine,
and sometimes livin' early just gives you more time.

WITH OR WITHOUT US THE
FUTURE IS HAPPENING.

TUNE IN.

Unlike Indian Hindu wisdom that offers states of
being and metaphysical paths to liberation, proverbs
are more rigid and self-stated. More African. Where
there's no sentiment or mysticism, and only
elephants mourn their dead, which is either by
starvation or predation.

MAN

UP

So much of life seems to come back to courage, doesn't it? Being willing to go one more step before you quit. One step deeper into your relationships, one step further in being faithful to yourself, to your God. What if everybody took one more step to salvage their marriage, to secure their own character, to not sell themselves short? One more step by enough of us can change the world.

THE VICTOR SEES THE LIGHT LAST.
THE FINAL BELIEVER WINS THE CROWN.
DON'T PULL THE PARACHUTE TOO EARLY.
FLY UNTIL YOU TOUCH DOWN.

CARVE AND BURN

the fat from the meat,
the wheat from the careless chaff.
In the name of transformation
die a little instead of completely.

Proverbs inherently admit that we believe there was
an author of Order behind Creation. They
acknowledge that what we do in this life matters
while we're here, and at the same time they accept
that what we do in this life has to do with what
happens to us in the next.

It is healthy for the soul
to put itself in a place not atop the food chain.
As you die not to feel the pain
don't determine discomfort as an enemy of your state.
It's often an ally to your progress.

EVERY

TIME

WE

STAND

TO

BE

CORRECTED

WE

ALSO

STAND

TO

BE

CORRECT.

When we talk about consequences, everybody immediately thinks they're only negative. In truth, consequences go both ways. With every decision, choice, and action, there will be a give with the take, a credit with the debit, something desirable will happen and something unpleasant will happen, something good and something bad. We don't give enough credit to the positive side of consequences, to the desirable outcome, to the good result, to what they can give us.

The universe is designed to kill us,
The world to rob our peace,
Unattainable for pride and physics,
Is a promise of belief.

Never meant to be on the menu,
We won't find it if we disengage,
Peace is a gift of God and Grace,
To reach it we must rage.

Bill Parcells, former coach of the New York Giants,
said, "If you want to be a head coach, get ready to
deal with six to eight big problems that you could
never have thought were coming every day." What
would happen if we all had in our consciousness that
every day is about solving six to eight problems we'll
never see coming? Life's hard. It's supposed to be.
That's the inevitable deal. And once we admit it, we're
more ready for it, and it's a lot easier to handle.

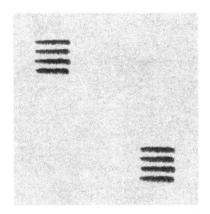

GOOD MAN

There's a difference between a good man and a nice guy.
A good man stands for certain ideals.
And when those beliefs are contested,
a good man is not a nice guy.

I wrote this one in the late '90s, just before I decided to stop doing the romantic comedies. People were always telling me, "Ah, man, you seem like such a nice guy." And hey, I got it; the rom-coms were entertaining and popular, and the men always ultimately acquiesced. But it reminded me of when I was a kid and the girls would say, "Oh, you're so cute," and I was just dying for one of them to say, "You're handsome." Aspiring to be just a nice guy is like short-sheeting yourself; you're a nice guy, but what do you stand for? The nice guy's easy to be around, but he goes along with everything. A good man's different. He has things he stands for. It's harder to be a good man.

I

I have faith in what I believe I *could*.
I speak of what I believe I *should*.
I do what I believe I *would*.

Give me the faith to believe
the confidence to speak
and the courage to do.

PROPAGANDA

The comfort and convenience you get from relying on the encore,
will pale in comparison to a great concert.
The lenient quick fix you keep lending yourself,
is pennies compared to the endless luxury you can afford.
The posture you pose in fifteen minutes of fame,
is nothing compared to the legend of your character.
The lies you tell may buy you some time,
but the truth will make you immortal.
The gifts you hoard and hide will make you jealous,
but the ones you share will show them how.
The sperm on your belly is child's play,
compared to the baby you can make with their mother.
The knowledge you keep will entertain your mind,
but the wisdom you give will light the way.
The thanks you expect will hold you entitled,
but the gratitude you give will breed freedom.
The time you save will get you there early,
but when you're on it, you'll never be late.
The steps you learn will win you a ribbon,
but the dance you do will keep you in rhythm.
The nightmare you have is for a whore,
and the wet dreams you make love to are yours.
The negative is singular, the positives are plural.
Please sell them as so.

GOOD REBEL

Goodness rebels bless us to be
more than obedient to Your law.
Even when consequences have no account
give us ear to heed Your call.

May we more than *do* good in Your name
may we *be* more in our breath.
Where we experience, express, and demonstrate You
in all that we attest.

Give us the courage to act in just,
to crave and need You in complete.
With unwavering lust for Your covenant love
to humbly seek you till we meet.

Amen

Lusting for love is a great lust. It does not mean
ridding yourself of carnal desires, but rather
persuading your passions into beliefs.

PREVENTION BEFORE THE CURE IS IN NEED.
WHERE COURAGE IS NOT OF REVENGE,
BUT OF SUFFERING TO SUCCEED.

WHEN REQUESTING ANYTHING
YOU DO NOT YET POSSESS,
THE ANSWER IS NO.
UNTIL IT IS YES.

SOLO MAN

Respect family.
See everyone as someone's child, sibling, and parent.
Respect them as such.
Love thy neighbor as thyself.

REGULATION

GAUGES

With an ebb and flow of consequences for
every decision made, calibrations are
necessary for every choice we make.
Meaning, if you make a profit in one place,
you're gonna get a debt in another. Seldom
are all systems running at peak
performance. So how do you keep what's
important to you in the black? The
measurements of importance in my life are
my health, my family, my marriage, my
career, and my relationship with God. I'm
always having to recalibrate and adjust the
gauges to maintain balance. My career's
taking off and taking all my time? *Whoops,*
relationship with my family and God starts
slipping into the red. My kids and I are each
other's favorite people and my six pack's
ripped? Probably need to spend more time
with my wife. And because I don't want to
let any of those go too far south, I have to
take inventory, and recalibrate. Remember
those Alpine car stereo equalizers in the
1980s? Life's a balancing act and you've
gotta keep re-tuning your equalizer to stay
out of the red.

REGULATIONS

Listen to yourself,
hear yourself,
learn yourself and mind.

Measure yourself,
train yourself,
referee yourself in kind.

Negotiate yourself,
invest yourself,
multiply yourself and scale.

Administer yourself,
accomplish yourself,
dare yourself from hell.

Own yourself,
exchange yourself,
pay yourself back.

IT'S GOOD WHEN YOUR
SUCCESS GOES TO YOUR HEAD.

AS LONG AS IT GOES TO YOUR
HEART AS WELL.

HEARTLINE.

I've been running from my soul
skating on the surface
seeking transformation
through transactions of a purchase.
It's a one way street to everything at all
a lead pipe cinch for not far to fall
it'll never get me high enough to see what's down below
I'm gonna need more elevation
to heartline my show.

This is another one that sums up a time when I was
famous and successful but dealing with a fear of
complacency. I had box office hits, was getting paid
great, everything was easy, what else did I need?
The problem was that not enough of it meant enough
to me. Yeah, I was *succeeding,* but was I making a
profit? I was looking for some courage to throw a
jackknife into my habitual rituals. I needed to bloody
my own nose, make a change.

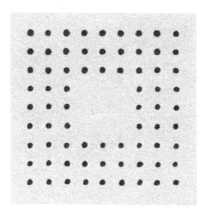

LEVERAGE

heights are worth the fear.
ladders are worth the climb.
fences are there to let us know.
And if you want to go to the edge when you're at the top,
start on your stomach.

ON THE OUTSKIRTS OF TOWN

on the outskirts of approval
a little closer to I don't need it
where my backyard has a lawn
and it's up to me to deed it

on the outskirts of permission
next door to nobody minds
down the road from conditions
and your word ties the bind

on the outskirts of the brewery
a little closer to cold beer
where if someone gives a listen
you give a chance to hear

where there's no hurry up to get there
and you don't have to wait in line
on the cul-de-sac of an apology
makin' things just fine

on the outskirts of clever snark
too busy lookin' down to find it
where an upright soul can swagger
with a lot of care to mind it

on the outskirts of ambition
and racin' in the rat
in between the divide
of I'll do *this if* you do that

on the outskirts of more money
as a pass to having class
where all you gotta be is you
as long as you're not an ass

on the outskirts of the dorks
a little closer to the nerds
where the traffic isn't jammin'
and the road's got room for swerves

on the outskirts of crime
a little closer to misdemeanor
up the road from arrested
where the sheets are a little cleaner

on the outskirts of pride
a little closer to your honor
catercorner to a good fight
further from you're a goner

on the outskirts of socialites
that never earned a callus
cozy in a cabin
that sleeps more like a palace

on the outskirts of illusion
with solid walls for me to lean
down the road from America
a little closer to the dream

on the outskirts of trendy
a little closer to classic
down the street from surgery
a little further from the plastic

on the outskirts of honkin' horns
a little closer to right-of-way
around the bend from stealin' to win
where work still makes your hay

on the outskirts of memberships
a little closer to general admission
with fewer motors on the water
cus the lake's still good for fishin'

on the outskirts of litigation
a little closer to common sense
up the road from trespassing
where you don't need a fence

on the outskirts of flamboyance
a little closer to need
off the cocaine highway
on the dirty road to weed

on the outskirts of rules
a little closer to choice
where you don't have to yell
for me to hear your voice

on the outskirts of 9 to 5
a little closer to when you do
where you're lookin' out for me
and I keep an eye on you

on the outskirts of edgy
but still on the banks
where manners are a currency
in the free trade of thanks

on the outskirts of revenge
a little closer to grace
where there's rhyme on the road
to reason for the race

on the outskirts of exhausted
a little closer to tired
where being good at what you do
keeps you from being fired

on the outskirts of most popular
a little closer to cool
where come one comes all
and doesn't suffer a fool

on the outskirts of re-recorded
a little closer to LIVE
a few more miles from the studio
a few doors down from the dive

on the outskirts of proof
a little closer to believe
where immaculate conception's
more easily conceived

on the outskirts of cynics
but still a little skeptic
where there's still moss on the stone
minus the septic

on the outskirts of long shadows
but closer to the shade
a zip code away from the mall
where retail's local made

on the outskirts of lyin'
a little closer to BS
snuggled up near nervous
but still further from stress

on the outskirts of disease
a little closer to sin
where gettin' where you're goin'
depends on where you been.

◆

I always go to a new place, and if I like it, I wanna
move there and get a spot right where I had a good
time—Main Street, Bourbon Street, Sixth Street,
Sunset Boulevard. But I stay there long enough and
I soon realize . . . No, actually, I don't want to live
on Tourist Attraction Avenue. I'd rather live on the
outskirts, a little further from the main drag and
draw. Austin, Texas, used to be on the outskirts of
town—the outskirts of Dallas, the outskirts of
Hollywood—but now it's a metropolitan city. I still
live there though, because to me it's still a village.

TIPS INCLUDED

When extra credit's included
credit doesn't get its due,
when more gives us less
the exchange rate's gone askew.

When amnesty's offered
going into the crime,
we're more bound to commit it
because there is no fine.

We start playing to tie
instead of going for the win,
when participation's the trophy
for every cow in the pen.

If I stay on the porch
because you picked up the slack,
when you look over your shoulder
I can't have your back.

If there is no curfew
we'll stay out all night,
no tab at our bar
we get drunk and start a fight.

All these long lenses
got us losing our sight,
you keep liftin' it for me
I'll lose all my might.

When a four-star duty
suits a six-star rate,
we take our hands off the wheel
and rely on fate.

Eating all we can
at the all-we-can-eat buffet,
gives us a 3.8 education
and a 4.2 GPA.

We steal from ourselves
and get away with the scam,
what's the measure of merit
with less give a damn?

These unlimited options
sure have me confused,
while all the conveniences
keep me properly lubed.

In this red-light district
with the whore of inflation,
the ROI's math
don't pay for vacation.

So let's just admit it,
this extra credit's quite a fluffer,
cus when the tip's included
the service will suffer.

PROJECTION

We see as far as we remember
forecast as far as we recall,
projection equals inventory
no matter how big or small.
Our expectations and estimations
plans and potentials,
are most clearly seen and supported
when measured by these credentials.
By the cache of our archives
accounts and evidence,
all in equal measure
of what's to come and what is hence.

The concept that we can only project into our future
as far as we can remember into our past came to
me after writing *Greenlights*. Never one who liked to
look over my shoulder, I was forced to deal with my
past for the first time. Only then was I able to
project further into my future, because for the first
time I was able to see further into my past.

YOUR FRIEND BEEN.

Never speak or think of any pain,
discomfort, or dislike that *was,* as if it is still.
Put it always in the past tense
and you block its path to prophecy.

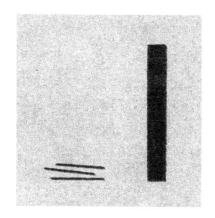

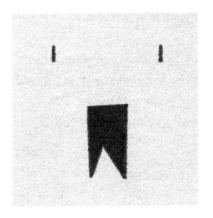

Cobra man say,

"If get bit, think like it small thing
so your heart beat slower so less
venom get to your body and you
live longer. If get bit and think it
big thing your heart beat faster,
and you die sooner."

LIFE AND CANDY CRUSH

Candy Crush teaches fiscal responsibility,
how to save and how to spend.
Where the hints and tips are helpful,
until you start to win.

Then comes the bad advice,
and their suggestions start to lie.
Because only *after* you win the prize,
do they blitz you with offers to buy.

It'll cost you the same price to open your piggy bank
for only half the gold that was there.
But you can start each game with a wheel to spin
just like you're at the fair.

You'll find it best to decline the first offer
in the barter of any exchange.
Because a better one will soon follow,
and you can win more games.

Candy Crush teaches time management,
how to make up your own mind in measured time.
That if you ask a friend for help
they'll usually be kind.

And if they help you once,
they'll probably ask you back double.
Because sometimes in life you can and do,
have to buy your way out of trouble.

LIFE'S A MIRACULOUS
JOURNEY OF FALSE
SUMMITS UNTIL THE END.

SURRENDER TO THIS FACT,
AND CLIMB UNTIL THEN.

HILLS

When they are no longer in our way but on it.
With their invitation to climb,
they're resistance our daily grind,
giving reason to our rhyme,
they slow us down to be on time.
And no one can take us home if we don't know where we're going.

I wrote this on a bike ride in Vietnam after I'd taken the long way home and was halfway up an excruciating hill to get there. Already exhausted with the sun quickly setting, I was between too far up to go back and not far enough up to continue, so I carried on. As I struggled to pedal through the pain, I realized, hills are just necessary parts of life's terrain, there for the climbing.

The last line's from the same trip when my buddy Woody Harrelson went to a bar in Haiphong at four P.M. and walked out twelve hours later. After getting in the back seat of a cab to head home, Woody realized he had no idea where or what the name of our hotel was. That's when the cab driver, who spoke very little English, turned around and said to him, "I cannot take you home if you do not know where you are going."

Never give up your right to do the next right thing.
This is how we find our way home.

PLACEBOS

Trying to entertain my way to heaven
with retail therapy, drugs, and attention
all in the name of a foolish game
called pains of life prevention.

Idols of ruse self-abuse
products for our spiritual degrade
on sale at every corner
easy to find and ready-made.

Apples in Eden's garden
success without the prophet
a chickenshit flyweight posture
a pouch without the pocket.

When winning this mortal game
means losing the immortal race
the quantity's over-qualified
the measurement misplaced.

Not a relay we can win today
this competition demands belief
it takes a lot of faith to play
for the trophy of relief.

Be scared,
but don't be afraid.

LOVE

STORIES

Love is a poem.

"Wanna go find some dandelions?
I'll pick 'em, you can blow 'em."

—Livingston, age four

REVEL IN THE POST.

(The consequences of good lovin'.)

Everything after and each other gets softer,
eyes, lips, shoulders, and the hips brushed by in passing.
The pain bruises without drawing the blood,
we hear, see, and feel the salts, sweets, and sunsets.
The tannins of the treble get off their tippy toes
and lounge in the hammocks with their more basser tones.
Quiet moments aren't so loud.
The air more dense as Mother Nature lends
a fresh side of the moon to light your face.
Magic hour stays up later,
the edges of your eyes grow peach fuzz,
and you don't miss your glasses.
Time slows until tardy is on it,
you hear virgin songs
from birds that have always sung,
and a thought becomes a mood
uninterrupted for the rest of the night.
She'll wear less makeup out to dinner,
you'll treat her like the queen she is and order a rib eye.
The sips on your cocktail will be smaller
so that your drinking can last longer.
You remember missing yourself this morning
because you weren't here,
and relish tomorrow's schedule which has no plans.
And even on a hot summer evening you can smell October
through the sweat where you left the windows open and forgot
    to shave.

MAY OUR HEART
CARRY OUR FEET.

AMEN.

Once a week I cry for thanks
so my soul can catch its breath.
Because when you're gone I'll miss you
I love you until your death.
Tears of joy for both hope and pain
to have and lose what I have left.

MEET YOU IN THE MIDDLE

At the edge of our property line,
on the border between where we're from,
I'll see your past, you'll see mine.
With a limit to lean on and hindsight,
it's here we'll get along fine.

TRUTH SLAVE

When the truth comes to visit
and her presence feels your peeve,
make sure to let her in
then never let her leave.

If it's a one-night stand you're out for
gone she'll be before first light,
but if forever's on her pillow
in your bed she'll stay all night.

Never easy to live with
because she's always in the know,
defending your court of conscience
when in the wind you blow.

Grow old with you she will
by your side and for all time,
good counsel she will give you
across the immortal finish line.

From tenant to friend to family
she'll get rooted in your veins,
a parasite of propaganda
that will infinitely remain,

true. to you.

PEOPLE WILL DIE IN YOUR LIFE
WHO YOU WILL KNOW

WOULD HAVE LIVED LONGER HAD
YOU BEEN A BETTER FRIEND

CERTAINLY

Out to confront instead of restore,
I've been confusing selfish for certain.
Locked behind my dictator's door,
the insecurity of combat's curtain.
Always competing for the win,
I need more care and consideration.
To make some space for sin to swim,
would be fair in correlation.
I know I'm seldom wrong,
but there's more than one way to be right.
Others deserve a chance to belong,
especially my wife.

STUMBLE FORWARD

we push, we pull,
sometimes pinched and wider than either

we expand, we contract
we look forward looking back

we're solid, we squirm
we argue, we confirm

we tell the truth, we lie
do what it takes to get by

minor chords and major threats
net incomes and gross assets

out of tune between right and wrong
until we stumble upon a song

BEST THING YOU CAN
DO FOR YOUR
MARRIAGE,

ONE WAY TO SURELY
GET AHEAD,

IS GET RID OF THAT
KING-SIZE MATTRESS,

AND SLEEP IN A
QUEEN-SIZE BED.

SELFISH

God, help me to
trust myself enough to rely on others
respect myself enough to honor others
be generous enough with myself to serve others
believe in myself enough to have faith in others
love myself enough to care for others
forgive myself enough to have compassion for others
convict myself enough to judge others
appreciate myself enough to thank others
listen to myself enough to hear others
know myself enough to learn from others
miss myself enough to stay home
be secure enough to leave
and pray enough to know You
Amen.

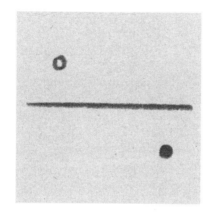

RHYME AND REASON

Gentle rain on Sunday
giving rhyme to my reason.
Laying ambition down to rest,
a lover for my season.
She whispers caution to my mind,
"Be gentle with tomorrow,"
when you put reason to your rhyme.

It's a bloody waltz on the wings of screaming eagles
and my animal's in a fight with God.
We claw and fight and spar in flight,
we court to the ground in bloody delight,
my battled will I defend till death,
as *"I love you"* spits from my last breath,
"Your unconditional love I can't deny!"
"I know" you whisper, and again we fly.

DAUGHTER'S BED

Need to lie down and rest my head,
think I'll take a nap in my daughter's bed.
Hopin' on a hunch it'll clear my mind,
slow down my clock, get me back on time.

What do I forgive and where's the buck stop here?
Been forty-eight days since I had a beer.
I ain't quit nothin', just hadn't had any since,
takin' a peek on the other side of the fence.

It's not any harder and it's just as easy,
spend a bit more time tryin' to please me.
Weary and unrested, the sun's goin' away,
and I'm stuck here just starting my day.

Take care of the kids, love on their mother,
look in the mirror, sometimes see another.
To see women as sisters and men as my brothers,
hopin' to pull it off here under these covers.

Here on the innocence of cleaner sheets,
a place where the pillow never cheats.
Where the nightmare this time is just a cold sweat,
not a reminder of an unpaid debt.

Cus sometimes we need to lie down and rest our head,
take a little nap in our daughter's bed.
Hope on a hunch it'll clear our mind,
slow down our clocks, get us back on time.

VALENTINE'S DAY

Too many white roses, not enough red.
"I wish you loved me as much as life," she said.
"One last time, is it yay or nay?"
And that's when my feet stepped away.

FUCKUPS,

DAYMARES,

WOBBLY,

LOST

&

LOOKIN'

I continually miss the mark, come up short, sin, and am not the man I aim to be—the father, the friend, the husband, the artist I aim to be. I don't like it, but I wonder: If we're not missing, coming up short, or sinning enough, maybe we aren't trying hard enough. Are we not venturing close enough to the front lines of life's battles? I'm not sure, but I don't believe that God wants us to stay warm and cozy in the even money exchange rate of doing just enough *not* to dare sin, failure, or coming up short. To leave this life and arrive home with fewer sins but less victories might even be a sin in itself.

I've also had plenty of times when the world's just not making any sense. Times when I've been lost in the haze, looking for the dream and not finding it because I couldn't see through my own fog. Sometimes we figure out what we should do by doing what we shouldn't enough times to get sick of it. You know how it is. We kiss that fire and walk away whistling enough times we're gonna eventually chap our lips and lose our tune. I suppose that's part of the existential struggle—that we gotta go deep enough into the pain to recognize we can't bear the existence. Far enough into the dark to come out the other side and see the light.

DREAM TEAM

Trying to get Truth to meet Honesty,
Honesty to hang out with Frank,
Frank to hook up with Jiminy Cricket,
and Jiminy Cricket to marry Desire.
And it'd be nice if they all got along for more than a couple of hours.

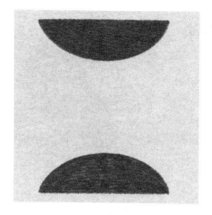

God,
I feel caught between trying to make heaven on earth
and trying to get to heaven after I leave here.
Do we get more heaven on earth by trying to get there?
Or do we get more hell on earth so we can?

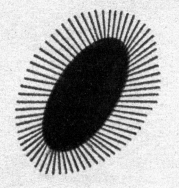

DAYMARES

Not the ones that haunt us
in the depths of each dark night
but the ones we have all day
that live out in the light.

The monsters we're afraid of
and don't dare look in the eye
the boogeymen we *should* believe in
but constantly deny.

The bad wolves we feed
the wounds we cut ourselves to bleed
the pets that we peeve
the lies we heed.

The addictions and pains
the murders and the shames
the blames and bad aims
the drains and false claims.

The abuse, misuse,
and counterfeit incarcerations
the proof we never had
before the condemnations.

The crimes we commit
and then falsely acquit
the evil we possess
but will never admit.

Dear God,

Seems my sight's getting in the way of Your sound,
so many signs You left me I never found.
When everything's significant there's no significance at all,
I'm down on all fours with nowhere to fall.

My eyes are crossed from lookin' past the clues,
reading back to front and missing the news.
With everything so certain it's all in doubt,
I'm upside down and inside out.

Looking for meaning in every detailed frame,
giving every particular its own Proper name.
Chasing every drop blind to the rain,
I'm paralyzed, confused, and manic in pain.

Not seeing the forest for this damn tree,
it's well past time to bend my knee.
So I can hear and witness Your tells and suggestions,
in the spiritual gym where You exorcise my corrections.

Back in the days when I used to smoke weed, it was Mexican dirt weed. The kind where you passed the joint around, laughed, got the munchies, and hopefully snuck off for some good sex.

Somewhere along the way, weed seemed to get on steroids, and instead of being a tiny toke of easy inspiration, it turned into a paralysis puff of fucking analysis. Suddenly, I'd find myself stuck for hours staring at that one grain in that one piece of wood in my ceiling rafters, thinking it was trying to tell me something important. It wasn't. Hell, one time I missed my own birthday party because I couldn't quit playing this one song over and over in my car. Yeah, for some reason, it seemed more important for me to listen to Janet Jackson's "That's the Way Love Goes" thirty-two times in a fucking row than to show up for the celebration of the day I was born.

If every dance step matters too much, we never find our rhythm. If we give every note too much credit, we'll never hear the song.

That's why I quit smoking.

I've been trying to criticize my way to superiority.
Exaggerating the faults of my neighbor.
Instead of biting my tongue I've been taking pride
in the applause of its uncharitable tune.
Forgive me, and at least give me the courage to
shut the fuck up instead.

We've all been caught putting other people down to
make ourselves feel better. Applauding louder for
their miss than our make. It's a false sense of
security we have, feeling better when other people
lose than we do when we win.

SPLIT DIFFERENTIAL

looking for things that I have seen,
on the outs and in the between.

opening drawers that I've opened prior,
this constant crying wolf's proof I'm a liar.

imagining places it's perfectly hidden,
just because it's gone does that mean it's forbidden?

believing it is where it's never been,
a penance I pay to atone for my sin?

running out of age to find what's mine,
believing I will if I have enough time.

And I don't.

TEMPTATION

High moon, midnight,
numb drunk, smoked up,
unkind with vile mind.
The vultures and hyenas are circling,
the soiled border between the carnal and my constitution.
Into my den of sin I'm about to invite them in,
when I see an albino armadillo irrigating my lawn,
and I realize it's time to tend my garden,
to fast and get hungry again,
to check in and choose so not to stay checked out and chosen.

THE MESS I MADE.

The mess I made
oops I did it again,
spilled my drink
of disease and sin.

Gonna take a while
to clean this up,
spilled more than I thought
emptied the cup.

Which was bigger than I remember
and filled to the top,
now it's dripping through the cracks
the wood's swellin' with rot. ⤳

Walked on the tab
didn't pay the bill,
the buzzards are circling
smellin' fresh kill.

The mosquitos are swarmin'
they love standing water,
happy to trade
a bite for their barter.

The flies are gettin' local
they smell something sweet,
it's gettin' shady and humid
and they like the heat.

The kitchen's a flood
the water's on the rise,
the hat's outta the rabbit
I lost my disguise.

Call 911
get the National Guard,
it's a hundred-year drought
and I'm watering my yard.

No time left to bluff
I need a wild card,
my damn glass broke
and my foot found the shard.

Now blood's in the water
sharks are on the way,
emergency landings
on the Hudson Bay.

I'd bend a knee to beg
but the bottom's too deep,
can't hold my breath that long
the price is too steep.

Too many affairs
too scared to marry,
I'd scream for help
but my voice won't carry.

The stars are laughing
at my expense,
no rain for me
I've made my last rinse.

The king of my castle
a circus for a clown,
in this mess I made
here where I'll drown.

Oops, yep, I did it again,
spilled my drink
of disease and sin.

NOT QUITE SURE HOW
TO DO IT WRONG.

BUT PRETTY DAMN SURE
I DIDN'T DO IT RIGHT.

FALLEN LEAVES

as night falls I rise
to give the sun its shade
the days end now I can sin
in this shadow that I've made

with nothing to do, up to no good's next
the witch pot brewed I'm under the hex
more than bored I'm losing my mind
this paranoia is mighty unkind

with the M and the E I'm in quite a bind
believing in lies that I'll never find
scratchin' till I bleed on the leg of my hind
this long night ahead's already a grind

all this confusion breeding illusion
nothing will stick, there is no fusion
crying wolf without an ear to hear my tear
I'm more than scared, I'm feral with fear

Like a black dog running from my shadow on a moonless midnight,
I'm shaking this tree so I can bark at the fallen leaves.

WHAT'RE YOU GONNA DO?

When the hand you played turns out to be a pawn
when you're lost in the weeds of your own lawn
when those you believe in have all moved on
and what you saved up for is all but gone.

When what you relied on becomes brand new
when the clouds are all gone and the sky's just blue
when your backstage pass is standin' in the cue
and you're too tired to rise and touch the mornin' dew.

When your showin' off quits causin' a swoon
when the music's over and you lost your tune
when the lady in your bed starts ridin' a broom
and you need to go to jail but they ain't got room.

When one's enough but you still want two
when your friend's no show and it's all on you
when you give up on forgiveness and start to sue
and there's no one left to blame, only you.

When you're high in the rise and you miss the dirt
when the hands that once soothed are now the ones that hurt
when you see evil and your eyes won't avert
and your million-dollar smile's turned into a smirk.

When you're bowin' on both knees cryin' at the pew.
when your body don't mind what your head tells it to do
when nobody's your boss, not even you
and you're lookin' back on it with your last view.

What're you gonna do?

I wrote this a few years ago after turning fifty. Something about that number made me think more about my mortality, my legacy, my relevance, and admit that the blue-eyed blonder days don't last forever. Yeah, something about turning fifty makes a man realize he's gonna be on the Thursday side of life's week one day, if he's not already.

FAITH

&

DOUBT

Part of the reason my faith isn't as strong as I wish it was is because of my pride. It gets in the way. Whether that's the pride I have for knowledge, pride for approval, or the pride I have for self-reliance, my need for certainty, vanity, and independence feeds my doubt and is keeping me from fully surrendering the way true faith requires.

I also think pride is the reason a lot of people say they're *"spiritual,"* instead of *"religious."* To have full faith, you have to throw pride aside.

DOUBT FAITH

In this life, in our mind, through our eyes, and on each day, doubt is logical and reasonable.
Faith is not.
Faith does not rid doubt, rather it carries us through it.
May our faith outshine our doubt.

SOMETIMES

Sometimes I pray for guidance
sometimes I bow in confession
sometimes I ask for courage
or to remember a learned lesson.

Sometimes I pray to unload
some bullshit that's weighing me down
sometimes I pray for forgiveness
to find grace behind my frown.

Sometimes I pray for change
and the courage to move on
to a place that's hopefully up
where I remember what is gone.

Sometimes prayer's just a conversation
with my conscience testing my creed
so the whispers of the Truth
can grow from thought to deed.

I pray to lean into my blind spots
to highlight the laws of beauty
To seek and correct my aims
with freedom and on duty.

To realize that the unseen
which I many times deem as opposition
is more often just the unknown
of a daring proposition.

146

We need skeptics, not cynics.
One's discerning, the other doesn't believe.

MORTAL REGARD IS A
CHEAP TICKET.

RAISE YOUR HEAD AND
YOUR EYES WILL FOLLOW.

DARE TO PLAY THE
INFINITE GAME.

SOME PEOPLE HEAR THINGS,
SOME PEOPLE DON'T.
SOME PEOPLE SEE THINGS,
SOME PEOPLE WON'T.

HEAVEN OR NOT

Tomorrow is not today's measurement when the misery is bad enough.

To the suffering, consideration is a privilege.

And that is part of what faith and religion are for.

To help those in misery hang on to a hope that will most likely not be served them in this life, to sell them belief and faith that they will be served in the next.

And what if there is nothing there? Nothing to hope for? No next?

I do not know.

Either way, in misery here or without a heaven there, not having any hope or faith in anything is a certain way to remain where you are forever.

But if you can find something that can keep you going, something, no matter how small, to look forward to and continually have faith in and chase?

Well, then your life here will be better than it is now, heaven or not.

HEAVYWEIGHTS

dangerously honest and intimidatingly true,
when they say *no* we say please,
when they say *uh oh* we say human.

what we got's not sold over the countertop,
there's nothing generic about our grade,
more than just our fault, it's how we're made.

how arrogant it would be to say we shouldn't,
or cry uncle that we're already done,
when what is read is what we wrote,
it's game over, we won.

it's scary stuff this believing,
mouth guard recommended, blood will be drawn,
committed to the life of us,
without insurance of the pawn.

it's gonna take all the courage we can must,
to give the credit where it's just,
and the grace to see each other in ourselves.

TODAY, MAY I BE AVAILABLE TO
SEE MYSELF AS GOD SEES ME

AND FAITHFUL ENOUGH TO
BELIEVE IT.

I BELIEVE THAT
FAITH IS THE ANSWER
IN THE END,

BUT FOR NOW ALL I
KNOW IS THAT IT
HELPS ON THE WAY
THERE.

UNTIL THEN, AMEN.

Hey God,

I know I make excuses for spending time with You,
and the other day before we talked,
I was so nervous I got a chew.

Can we hang out while I'm Peter Pan?
Is that too much freedom for Your guiding hand?
Is it all or none, a monk or a bum?
I feel like Mr. In Between.
And maybe that's what I am.

By the way, does it count when I talk to you while
    drinkin' at the bar?
Help me be humble enough to seek You
and brave enough not to cower.

Amen

I wrote this in 1999, when I was having trouble
believing in myself and forgiving myself at the same
time. I was trying to work out how I could admit I was
a sinner and forgive my sins, and how and when those
concessions were a cop out. Still working on it.

There's no such thing as an atheist.

We all believe in something, even if
that something is nothing.

And just because it's signed anonymous
doesn't mean it has no author.

SUNDAY.

A DAY TO BOW,
PRUNE, PIDDLE,
AND TEND.

AMEN.

COMPASSION,

FORGIVENESS

&

RAINING

GRACE

Now, I'm the first one to say that if I've done you wrong, sincerely apologized, and you've forgiven me, then my first order of business is to start doing whatever I can do not to have to say *I'm sorry* again. At the same time, if we have any ideals about how the world should be, about how we should act, we need to understand the value of compassion and forgiveness to get there. To some extent, we have to believe in rehabilitation. Some of us screw up because we're ignorant and just don't know better. Some of us know exactly how and why we screwed up and still want to make genuine amends for our behavior. I believe that if someone truly wants to seek reconciliation for their poor behavior, we should give them a chance. Who are we to say no to a second chance if our offender recognizes their wrong and comes to us with a heartfelt and accountable plea?

Forgiveness is on the way to grace. Grace is amnesty. You get grace when you understand that you don't deserve it. When none of it matters, and it all does at the same time. Grace is the place between self-reliance and surrender.

As well, forgiveness is good for us. Because when we don't forgive, the anger and spite we hold against our perpetrators can make us physically, mentally, and spiritually ill. Literally. Even when that perpetrator is ourself.

So here's to the sick getting healthy, and the healthy not getting sick.

"I love everybody in the universe except the bad guys.
And thank you, God, for bad guys,
because we can still make them into good guys."

—Vida's prayer, age five

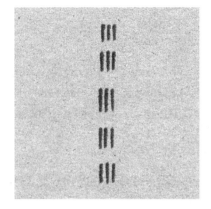

Forgive me, I'm sorry,
for the guilt of give a damn,
insane, a sinner, just who I am.
A repeat offender,
stuck right where I've been,
a certified transgressor,
over and over again.

Stress and guilt are necessary. It means we give a damn. I could be jealous of people who sleep well through the night after whatever offense they've committed, but I'm not, because that would mean I don't give a damn.

If someone lies, cheats, or steals,
the guilt of their crime is fact.
Do not deem them a *liar, cheater,* or *thief,*
instead, just condemn the act.

If someone sins against you,
forgive and pray for them each day.
And even if they don't repent
continue in this way.

This does not mean you should trust them.

LET GO TO CLIMB

HANG ON TO FORGIVENESS

CAN YOU FORGIVE ME, GOD?
CAN YOU FORGIVE? GOD?
CAN YOU FORGIVE GOD?

FORGIVE ME FATHER FOR I KNOW WHAT I DO

I design for ease and comfort,
but the comfort does not agree.
With no resistance to overcome,
I need self-service to be free.
A defining line from then,
a connecting thread to now.
Seeking stones in the field,
to make my road more rocky to plow.
Give me chaos to make order of,
a need to break a sweat.
To suffer for significance,
a beating to pay my debt.
A wobbly glutton I am,
I've lost my compass in this haze.
I sing songs and speak in tongues,
but only advertise Your ways.
Until I am tired,
sick with guilt from my presumption.
An uninvited guest I am,
overserved with my consumption.
Now I search for gravity,
please ground me Father fast.
Where proof can show its face again,
and I can look in the mirror and ask,

for forgiveness.

God, give me another sip of forgiveness
before I am drunk with resentment.
The sip allows salvation, but the drink is gonna kill me.

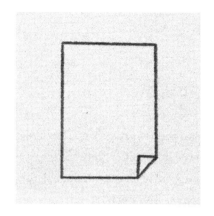

THE OTHER DAY I WROTE GOD A LETTER.

God,
forgive me, I'm trying.

And God replied,
"Thank you. I would rather you arrive
late to my house sweating, in a pair of
runners and a hoodie, than arrive
early elsewhere in a tuxedo."

UNTIL NOW

The patience of grace is not passive,
no, grace does not forget.
Knowing the past was all part of the plan,
she's never lost a bet.
Pressing on with urgency,
she always keeps her vow.
Knowing every day is the longest time,
and forever was until now.

AMEN

When responsibility becomes devotion
mandates become a choice
privilege turns to pride
and freedom hears your voice
honor becomes invitation
solitude gives you rest
hope dances with grace
and divinity serves you blessed

Dear God,
My carnal desires multiply and compress
piled high they bear down on top of my chest
their tower I need to topple and fall
so I can catch my breath and heed your call.

The lines and all the lies I tell
the ones I don't believe but sell
I'm lost and blind and can't seem to see
with nowhere to go's no place to be.

Looking for invitation to reunite and connect
an offer from the mirror for a chance at respect
I could use an early winter to warm this chill
a deal without the devil to settle my bill.

I need to get back my anonymous soul
whatever it takes I'll pay the toll
where the world is flat again and finally new
when the weight is gone and I'm closer to You.

Bound by the woven crimson thread of grace,
where I know, show, and see you in my own face.
Please.
Amen.

IS THE WEIGHT
WORTH THE WAIT?

TO MY FRIEND THE RAIN

Thank you for keeping my mind from the race,
for the damper on my ambition.
With you I care less for time or space,
instead I bow my head and listen.
To the thoughtful whispers of my soul,
as they dance to the tune of your trickle.
Where I see myself clearly in this world,
that you remind me is so fickle.

IN SPITE OF

Help me to have faith that the purpose of grace
is to show others the grace I've been shown.
That because we've already won the race
we accept again to win what is known.
Competing now to set the pace,
to be generous with what we own.

Not because we are good enough, but in spite
of the fact that we're not.
Amen.

AMERICAN

DREAMS

LOST

TO

FIND

The American dream is a promise for the opportunity to at least fail, and possibly succeed. Seems like the path to this dream is more undefined now than it's ever been. To those among us who don't believe in it and say, "It's not real," I say to you: "At least America's still trying." That's simply not true in so many other countries. So, whether you think it's a dream or an illusion, if nothing else, it's the best nightmare available.

This is about a time when I was in
Marfa, Texas, and had to go to
virtual court to get a restraining
order on a stalker.

STREAMERS IN THE HALL OF JUSTICE

Felt fresh this mornin' cus I was headed to court,
off to see a judge about a fact distort.

Seems a young lady claims we made a baby,
that never happened and I don't mean maybe.

Left an hour early so I'd be sure and have time,
for pullin' over to write these rhymes in my mind.

Followin' the line on my GPS,
I passed town square and found the address.

To my surprise it wasn't a courthouse at all,
it was an abandoned library with streamers in the hall.

In the shade of the water tower, cross the street from the fair,
odd place for judge and jury, and no one was there. ⤳

Then a masked lady appeared with a chair and table,
she seemed to be prepared, willing and able.

So I took a seat, a deep breath to get stable,
wonderin' if this was a joke or a fable.

Then the lady with the veil she gave me a code,
said "do what that says and follow your nose."

So I opened up my device and put the password in,
showed up in some place that I'd never been.

No a ruse it was not, I was where I was meant,
a virtual court across the country is where I was sent.

People were scrambling the place was a zoo,
I wondered aloud what myself was into.

"Turn off your mic!" I heard a loud voice roar,
"We'll let you know when you can have the floor."

So I muted my speaker, sat back and had a listen,
everybody was dealin' and backdoor dissin'.

Hoodscoopers, date rollers, wannabes, and overlaps,
as the clerk of the circus did his best to herd the cats.

Your honor was absent and so was the judge,
silly me for thinkin' litigation held a grudge.

An hour passed and so did the train,
good thing we sharp scheduled this waitin' game.

Not sure it's gonna happen but I'm here and ready,
no reason to be on time when the crime's this petty.

The prosecution needed tech support,
the lady accusing me never showed in court.

I guess the truth was above her station,
but the show went on, in CONtinuation.

While the clerk kept jugglin' a few people took a nap,
until he shared the local news from his earthquake app.

"The state of California gets two hundred a day!" he stated,
compared to this forum that's a crisis abated.

Even more confused now bout my day in court callin',
at least I know now why my chandeliers keep fallin'.

Next thing I know a voice says, "Raise your hand!
swear on the truth before you take the stand!"

And soon as I stated "yes I do,"
the judge asked me to confirm, "Are you *you*?"

And since I was, and still am,
it was an easy answer to get out of the jam.

Before it even got started there was not a further question,
"restraining order granted!," and that ended the session.

Well, that was a success, just not the way I expected,
makes me more suspicious of those we've elected.

Took two years to get the case to this court,
where his honor laid the law down without retort.

The verdict was swift, took less than a minute,
that's a whole lotta prep to just be handed the pennant.

This litigation gig, it seems quite the racket,
costs a lot of money just to see if you can hack it.

Cus when the fist grabs the gavel,
court's adjourned, and case dismissed.

Due process is the ass
that you do to get it kissed.

Good thing the courtroom was in an abandoned library,
with streamers in the hall of justice.

IF YOU CANNOT STOP THE LIES,
BECOME LESS GULLIBLE.

PEP RALLIES

I'm not a fan of fairy-tale liberal commentary,
nor the right-wing dictate semper fi.
I prefer a documentary,
where the truth unfolds on the fly.

I revere politics and the politician's position of
service, but the more I'm around the political arena,
the more I see it's about negotiations, compromises,
party preservation, and pep rallies. I wish it was
more about selling beliefs, standing on principles,
sacrifice, and showtime. Hell, that's what I wish for
myself and everyone else as well.

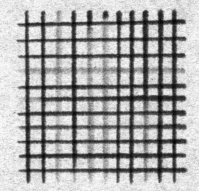

BLESSED ARE THE PEACEMAKERS

If a peacemaker brokers other people's values,
is it peacemakers we should be?

In a world for better or worse,
we sure see good and evil,
black and white, wrong and right,
our definition of what's legal.

Without considering the spirit,
so quick to condemn the word,
too insecure to understand,
only fighting to be heard.

Religion can't find a common ground,
because of its moral obligations,
rational people do it every day,
so why not neighborhoods and nations?

Seems we're more doctrinaire than ever,
all addicted to upheaval,
maybe we're here to broker better or worse,
and let God deal with good and evil.

AMERICA, YET.

On the American dream, Langston Hughes wrote, America is a "land that has never been yet."

America is a land that, like any individual with the ambition and will to improve, be better, and succeed—will never arrive.

Always on our way, America is a dream that is constantly updated, yet never realized. A place that will never be, yet.

The hero we chase, America is the heavenly place we seek. Our transcendent and better selves that we will never catch, where we improve and will never be our best, because we have the courage to continue the pursuit.

America is where we fight for equal opportunity and will never acquire it, where we seek justice and will never meet its measure, where we pursue righteousness and will still be wrong. The mountaintop we will never crest, yet continue to climb, the place where we have to and never will, the unattainable dream in the land of opportunity to chase it. That's America.

As Americans in America, we must be dreamers in our land of dreams, never satisfied members of the marathon that has no finish line, with an unquenchable thirst believing in and forever chasing ideals which we will never attain, united in ascension as a nation and a people who refuse to stop growing.

This is the American dream, our country's promise. Eternally unfulfilled, permanently in process, staying in the race, committed to the chase. Now and forever, yet.

GOD'S NOT POLITICS.
GOD IS PROGRESS.
AMEN.

SUNRISE

INTENTIONS

&

ALL-DAY

APPRE-

CIATIONS

*"Go back to bed and don't come out of your
room until you're ready to see the rose in the
vase instead of the dust on the table!"*

—my mom

I don't like waking up in the morning
feeling like I'm in a race *against* time. I like
starting my day feeling *on* time, and
grateful that I have another chance to live
and get what I want. So, before I get up, I
take a moment to check in with my mind,
body, and heart to see how I'm feeling.
How did I sleep? Where's my head? Am I
relaxed or anxious? Then I choose to
determine my frequency and approach to
the day ahead. Which lens do I want to see
the world through today? If I can choose
an outfit, I can damn sure choose my
outlook. When I take this initial intention
upon rising, it creates a subconscious
rhythm to the way I give and take
throughout the rest of my day, like a
soundtrack I can dance through life to, or
a score for the documentary I'll be living
out over the next twenty-four hours.

And it starts with baseline gratitudes.

Ahhh, morning morning!
How good it feels to be rested.
Where I see and accept the beauties given me for free.

Wake up in the morning and stare at the sun
until seven sneezes arise.
Then catch your breath and set your sacrum
until a yawn waters your eyes.

TODAY, GIVE ME THE HEART TO
KNOW WHAT FEELS RIGHT,

THE MIND TO ARGUE IF IT DOESN'T,

AND THE GUT TO DECIDE WHAT TO
DO FROM THERE.

I wrote this in Hollywood, 1994. With no agent,
sleeping on a friend's couch, and 2,000 bucks to my
name, I felt like I was running out of time. I was
trying to convince myself to be patient, be cool, to not
be in a rush—that I was on time, and not behind it.

As the son of what influences my character,
my thinking and my deeds,
may I align my mind, mouth, and sight,
as the spirit thinks, speaks, and sees.

CHEERS

Here's to making a better life for my children
while not missing the truth and beauty of my own.
To being inherently generous and properly lenient
while keeping my heart from being for loan.

As a man with no country here on earth
help me navigate the gray with grace.
May I welcome, see, feel, and share
listen and learn without haste.

To need what I want and want what I need
look and feel as I feel and I look.
May I drink to remember not to forget
the sins your sacrifice took.

amen

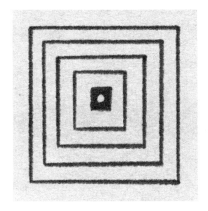

Turn your knowledge into wisdom,
know yourself.
Turn your wisdom into philosophy,
mind yourself.
Turn your philosophy into poetry,
rhyme yourself.
Then turn your poetry into song,
and dance.

MATTERING MATTERS

Dear God,

May what matters to me be what matters to You
May that matter determine what I do

May my struggle matter more than my strife
May death matter more than this life

May forgiveness matter more than revenge
May restraint matter more than my binge

May my wants matter as much as my needs
May my thoughts matter less than my deeds

May the truth matter more than the lies
May the hows matter as much as the whys

May the guest matter to the host
May the center matter to the coast

May the cheers matter to the toast
May the humor matter to the roast

May the living matter to the ghost
May less matter to the most

May earn matter more than deserve
May the steel matter to the nerve

May space matter to time
May the heart matter to mind

May the risk matter to the leap
May letting go matter to keep

May the spirit matter to our voice
May options matter to our choice

May what we say matter to mean
May our sight matter to what is seen

May rhythm matter to my muse
May finding matter when I lose

May should matter to must
May love matter to lust

May righteousness matter to just
May our word matter to trust

May laws matter to the offense
May borders matter to the fence

May money matter to spend
May prayer matter to the bend

May what's broken matter to mend
May the credit matter to lend

May memory matter to libation
May fun matter on vacation

May help matter to the holler
May prudence matter to the collar

May science matter to prediction
May dreams matter to fiction

May ignorance matter to abuse
May pardon matter to the excuse

May direction matter to the pace
May debate matter to the case

May heaven matter to seek
May patience matter to the meek

May our vows matter to I do
May the horizon matter to our view

CHOICE AND JUDGMENT ARE NOT
INHERENT OPPRESSIONS,

UNJUST AND CRUEL TREATMENTS ARE.

CONFINE YOURSELF TO THE LETTER
AND THE PRECEPT MAY BE LESS,

BUT IF YOU CONSIDER THE SPIRIT,
WORD AND INTENTION WILL CONFESS.

This is inspired by 2 Corinthians 3:6: *He has made
us competent as ministers of a new covenant—not of
the letter but of the Spirit; for the letter kills, but the
Spirit gives life.*
　　I believe we should care less about the letter of
the word and more about the spirit of how it was
spoken and the meaning behind it. Intent matters. The
word itself is merely the alphabet in a certain order,
but the spirit in which it is spoken is substance.

GIVE ME THE COURAGE TO EMBRACE THE GRACE
THAT I WILL NEVER ARRIVE.
THAT ONCE WE UNDERSTAND WE DON'T DESERVE IT
IS WHEN IT WILL PROVIDE.

Doers climb the wrong
mountains well.

Dreamers climb the right
mountains but aren't at
home on hills.

Doers help dreamers climb
more mountains.

Dreamers help doers climb
the right ones.

P.S.

Cheers to having the courage to
search for our own heaven on earth.

To understanding that the seeking is
as close as we can get to finding it.

To *Yet*—a tough place to gain, fickle
to hold, a daily toil of constant
pursuit, yet, a privileged path.

just keep livin', Amen.

ACKNOWLEDGMENTS

Thank you to:

Meister Eckhart; Mali, Africa;
Bob Dylan; and Brother Christian.

King Solomon, Pastor Dave Haney,
Lord Byron, and R. L Burnside.

Jack Kerouac, Hunter S. Thompson,
Robert Louis Stevenson, Rumi, and
John Prine.

Matthew Elblonk, Gillian Blake, Matt
Inman, Nicole Perez-Krueger, as well
as my wife, Camila, for taking the time
to make me write this book.

And finally to a few late, great mentors
and muses of mine, Don Phillips,
John Chaney, and Penny Allen.

"SOIL"

What wretched extent has our life bowed to today?
When will it end? When shall it begin?
Our endless judgements that brandish the sin.

Ignorant minds of the fortunate man
Blind of the fate shaping every land

Drifting day by day upon selfish wings of his past
Only seeking the wines of his narrow-minded cask

Love .... provide us a chance to cure the social disease
Or excessive infections have we never to believe?

As biased pasts rule unfortunate futures
Living adversities of both heaven and hell
Why the flame reaches higher is so hard to tell

No cell, no home, city, state nor land
The untold doom bleeds throughout every hand

The shrouded wounds sweat the pain unknown
Of so many; Premier, as kings upon the throne

Self-destruction of the blind awaits in the range
The naive dwelling of the endless unchanged

The unaware return to the palace of the benighted
I to shall reunite; primarily delighted

But one thing, infallibly, I will never remain,..
....
.. ..

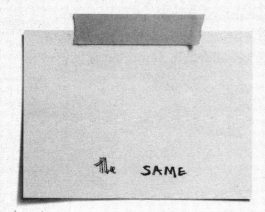

the SAME

1-1-89

As this book was about to go press, I found
this poem. I wrote it when I was eighteen
years old, in an Australian bathtub, strongly
considering being a monk, already using
poetry to try and make sense of this life.

ABOUT THE AUTHOR

Academy Award–winning actor and #1 *New York Times* bestselling author **Matthew McConaughey** is a husband and a father, an eternal optimist, a hopeful skeptic, and a man of faith who believes that we should all start sellin' Sunday morning like a Saturday night.

McConaughey is a professor of practice at the University of Texas at Austin and co-owner of the Austin FC soccer club. He and his wife, Camila, founded the just keep livin Foundation, which is dedicated to helping boys and girls transform into good men and women through programs that teach the importance of decision-making, health, education, and active living. McConaughey resides with Camila and their three children in Austin, Texas.